Love & Other Anxieties

Karaline Alessia

AOS PUBLISHING, 2021

AOS POETRY, 2021

ISBN: 978-1-9991105-4-3

Cover Design: Joey Cournoyer

Illustrations: Katherine Neal

Visit AOS Publishing's website:
www.aospublishing.com
Printed in Canada

Voler

Without wings, we must let faith guide us to places
beyond the clouds.
Blindly, but unquestionably, it will spring us forward
into worlds unimaginable.
We dreamed of days where failures were distant
memories in our thoughts.
We believed we would fly.
So, we did.

Pensées

Intertwined, quiet smiles.
Loud hearts, calm minds.
Under these stars, stay a little while longer.
You reminisce on better days
while I mend your broken thoughts of now.

Burnt toast, warm coffee,
don't your memories taste the same?
Stop living in the past.
That's where all the sad people go.

Trying to rebuild the puzzle of yesterday,
yesterdays are so good to you.

I'm missing a piece.

Rêves

Dreams are the gateways to the love we cannot grasp.
I've lived a thousand lives with you, each one
bringing me deeper in.
For just a moment,
I can feel your fingertips brushing my forehead
ever so gently.
We are young and in love,
but the sunlight carries the truth.
The dawn of a real day,
and I patiently wait until we meet again.

Âme

Books hold the souls of the broken hearted.
Heartfelt stories are written by lost love
and unfelt emotions.
The tear stained pages eventually dry,
but the words remain forever.

Nuages gris

Reminiscence, nostalgia,
blurry thoughts.
The word love was overused,
thoughtfully abused.

Glimmering sunlight of hope,
it peeks through grey clouds.
Staring longingly out a blurry window…
The word love was overused.

Couronne

Fix your crown girl, stand it up straight.
Eyes wide, fists clenched,
this world wasn't made for your strength.

Hold your crown girl. They'll try and take you down.
Stomp on the ground they think you don't deserve.

Wear your crown girl, and wear it proud.
You are the queen of this empire.
Wear it loud.

Yeux

Her mind's eye was radiant and blue,
searching for a home in the ruins.
Lost in a forest of thoughts,
wondering just how she ended up here.
Luckily, she found something familiar on the trail.
She found four walls inside your heart,
and since that day, she never left.

Petite fille

The little girl who lives inside me,
she gets nervous at parties,
and wonders why she's not at home with mommy.

How did I get here, in this office doing work?
Don't they know little girls should be at home
with their heads buried in a book?

Please don't ask me to come -
I can't.

I'm a little girl, I won't know how to act.

The little girl inside me won't let me grow,
so I'm trapped here,
at home.

Home.

home.

Toi

You look in the mirror,
frowning as you eye yourself up and down.
You cover up with big sweaters
to hide your extra pounds.
You don't stop to talk for too long,
afraid they'll see the sadness in your stomach.
Should you have worn this today?
'Only wear big sweaters',
you tell yourself.

//

He looks at you in the mirror,
smiling at your curves.
He wonders why you cover up so much.
'Stay a little while longer', he thinks.
'Stop hiding yourself in those big sweaters',
he wants to say.

If only you could see yourself through his eyes.

Pluie

Rainy days are for late mornings in bed,
sipping burnt coffee,
and telling you how much
I loved the way you looked
last night.

Claire de lune

The moon looks down and sighs.
Why can't she see how beautifully she shines?

Suivre

I will lead.
I will carry you into the midnight fire.
When all is burnt to dust,
I will build you up.
As the fire dies out, and the leaves whisk away -
I will lead.

Écoute

Never allow the one shallow voice,
among all those in the choir of hope,
to question your abilities.

Ivre

We are all drunk on the idea that love alone can save us.

La neige

In a moment of quiet solitude;
Snowy air and soft whispers -
I feel infinite.

Livre

Read for your mind,
your soul,
and for your sanity.
Books transport you to the world you wish you lived in,
letting you escape your reality for hundreds of pages.
If only we could step inside
and run away with the faeries,
leaving behind the enemies
that live too close for comfort.

Suffisance

My mind, my fears and my anxieties
find their peace when you remind me that
I am enough -
and if I am all that you need in this life,
that will be enough.

La magie

Magic can be found in every thought,
every word,
and every corner.
All we must do to find it,
is Believe.

Soulagement

In the midst of the busyness, of the chaos,
of the fast-paced life we lead -
I remember that I can find solace
in you.

Le coeur

We are so often blinded by
superficial distractions,
that we forget about the
little things in life.
We forget the true impact
we can have
on the world.
We forget the good we have
in ourselves to give.
We forget that life is nothing
without love,
without individuality,
without heart.

Amour

To love is to act selflessly,
and to cherish each stolen moment.
But to be loved -
that opens your soul.

Grand amour

In this lifetime,
and into the next,
your greatest love
will also be your biggest regret.

Luciole

Fireflies light up the night sky,
and I can't stop thinking about how much I love you.
Skip on the rocks,
but don't touch the ground !-
I couldn't if I tried.
I'm so high on the idea that you could
love me, too.

Anxiety is my Demon

Frozen fingers,
I can't seem to move.
The devil's in my head and he's made a home out of me.
The road seems long,
but the journey's never ending.
I can't seem to find my way.
Holding onto the anchor but I'm drowning with it.
The devil's in my head and he's not leaving.

Merci

I've made terrible decisions in love.
I've fought for hands I should have never held.
I've longed for a touch that burnt my skin black.
I've watched the clock tick as I waited to be loved.
And when the clock struck twelve,
I closed my eyes and started again.

You are not a choice.
You never were.
You are the only way I know how to live.
You hold my soul and send sparks down my spine.
The clock stops at 11:59.

Amour non réciproqué

Unrequited love.
Or is it?
I told you to leave because you needed better,
but truly I couldn't stand waking,
knowing you'd drink your morning coffee without me.
I told you to leave because it'll do you some good
to see the sunlight,
but really I couldn't stand to see you watch the moon,
while you thought about someone else.
Your heart is breaking?
Mine's already broken.
I told you to leave.
I didn't really mean it.

Your heart is breaking.
Mine is already broken.

Envie

The reason they look at you through
envy coloured eyes,
is because they hate the way they feel inside.
They are waging a war against
spiteful feelings of inadequacy,
and each time they pull out the sword,
they lose to jealousy.
They watch as you move with grace,
craving friendships and bonds,
but they are trapped inside a dangerous mind,
trying to escape every time.

Recommencement

Holding on to hate-filled words,
your kindness goes unnoticed.
You wonder why she listens to them tell her
she's not enough,
when you constantly remind her how
she makes your life better.
She swallows their words and ingests
their thoughts of her,
but she forgets how much you admire her.

Late at night, she thinks about it,
about everything you've said.
For a second,
even less,
she considers it.
She hugs you when you're sleeping,
and whispers 'thank you' when
she thinks you can't hear it.

But the morning sun brings out all of her insecurities.
She can see them in plain sight.

And so, we begin again.
Holding on to hate-filled words,
your kindness goes unnoticed.

Joue avec moi

Let's fly on the swings and sing with the birds.
Follow me down the rocky path, I promise it'll be fun.
Stay inside and watch cartoons on rainy afternoons.
We've seen this one a few times before, but it doesn't
matter when we're together.

Now the little ones have all grown up, but I'm still here
swinging and singing.
They've all gone to work but I'm still here.

Why have they stopped playing with me?

Ne m'oublie pas

You changed me.
In ways you'll never know.
You made me stronger.
Wiser.
And made me feel a love I didn't know.

You will grow up.
And you may forget some of the things I said.
But I will never forget you.

I will never forget the way you smiled
on a Monday morning,
eager to tell me about your weekend.

I will never forget the tears falling down your face
as you realized,
this is the end.

I will never forget you.

And I hope you won't forget me.

An ode to my first class.

Tu es jolie

You don't know you're pretty.
People forgot to tell you that you were pretty
when you walked into the room.
Instead they stared and laughed as you quietly sat down,
crumbling on the inside.

Somebody forgot to tell you that you were pretty,
so you wake up each morning trying your best
to avoid the mirror.

They forgot to tell you that you were pretty,
so you turn away when you feel as though
their eyes are on you.

What they didn't tell you was that pretty
doesn't matter so much.

It doesn't really matter at all.

Because the people that matter the most,

know your beauty inside.

Feux

There's a fire inside you,
And they keep trying to put it out.

The fire inside you burns bright-
Flames ablaze, destroying all your tragic thoughts.

And they keep trying to put it out.

Don't let them put it out.

Amour perdu

When the audience leaves,
and the lights turn off,

when the music fades,
and the curtains close,

what do you have left?

When the doors lock shut,
and you can't go back,

what do you have left?

What did they make you feel, all those months long?

Before they waved goodbye, and gave you one last look.

What did they make you feel?

What do you have left?

I hope you have love left.

Se souvenir

Remember me not by my name,
or by the way my hair moved in the wind,
but by the look in my eyes when I told you
it was finally over.

Jalousie

While you're busy hating other women for their
bright-eyed smiles and pretty faces,
I'll be building up our female empire -
Stronger together but you can't help your inner,
slithering jealousy.

She's not beautiful,
She's not skinny

Enough.

You tell yourself while you drown in your tears of envy.

Wouldn't your life be easier if you brought other
women up to the top instead of trying to bring them
down with you in your crumbling castle?

Her beauty doesn't make you ugly.

Your malicious thoughts do.

Forte

You can't help but want what she always had:

Strength.

Volé

Love is fun when it's not stolen.
Close your eyes and pretend he has been yours
all this time.

We both know that will never be true.

Détruire

The real tragedy is the desire you felt to destroy the one person who was there for you all this time.

Elle

Shades of black cloud your thoughts -
stuck in the same old routine again.
You wake up and wonder when the streetlight
will turn green.

You can't keep running in circles.

Grey coloured glasses because all you see is rain -
you can't remember when the world was pink.
You were ready to lose the fight against
this thing we call life.

But then you met her.

Vrai amour

Do you watch your life back like a movie?
Do you think about all the words you left unsaid
in the car?
Alone,
because you're too afraid to speak your mind?
Come along boy -
I'll show you what real love is all about.

Tarte aux pommes

Apple pie and sunny skies remind me of
why I loved you in the first place.

Soleil

Even grey skies have a sun hiding amongst them.

L’entendre

She looks down and hates what she sees,
but she knows they’re tired of hearing it.

She wishes that just once, she’d eye herself in the mirror
and not pick out every little detail
she can’t stand to look at anymore.

But she knows, they’re tired of hearing it.
Heaven knows, they’re tired of hearing it.

She’s tired of thinking about it.

But the scale won’t let her sleep
and that food she shouldn’t have eaten
keeps her awake at night.

They’re tired of hearing it.

Heaven knows,
she knows.

But they don’t know that she dreams of all the old
clothes that don't fit just right,
and they don’t know that she wonders why she can’t
look in the mirror

and just once,
only once,

like what she sees.

They're tired of hearing her tell herself
she's not thin enough.
She doesn't look nice in that dress.

They wonder why she just can't get over it.

But the dinner from yesterday keeps her awake at night,
and that workout she didn't do
eats away at her at night.

They're tired of hearing it.

Maybe you just need to listen.

One.

More.

Time.

Tell her something nice,

one more time.

Tell her again that she's beautiful.
She's not tired of hearing it.

Te détruire

Staring straight into the sun to admire it
for all its beauty,
but instead I shield my eyes away.

Sometimes the things we want most,
destroy us instead.

Sentiment

Felt in the soul,
but lost in translation,
she never told you how she felt.

You left that day and the sun never shone the same.
She should have told you how she felt.

You're doing better now
and perhaps so is she.
But she thinks to herself on warm summer nights,

that she should have told you how she felt.

Amis

Friends come and go,
even the ones you thought would stay.

Sometimes it's better that way.

Trust me,
it's better that way.

Écrire

He writes the words unspoken
after he walked away from your doorstep
wondering if he should have
kissed you that night.

New Orleans

Hot summer days, even hotter summer nights.

The music plays and I close my eyes.

Spirits fly while old stories are being told -

At every corner,

lie empty whisky cups

in front of busy voodoo shops.

Tell me my future.

When will I meet the love of my life?

I think I already did.

Drinking ourselves out of our stress-filled minds.

My heart was stolen on Bourbon Street.

Stormy Seas

Awake at night,
lying next to you,
is soundless.

Remembering a time when we barely knew each other.

You called me by my name and I grabbed your hand.
They are all fleeting moments in my mind,
running like a movie I never want to stop watching.

I can see the outline of your face in the moonlit room.
Love was not meant to be simple,
but I wouldn't travel these stormy waters

with anyone else but you.

Pretend

Let's play pretend.
Let's pretend to move away from here
and start a new life.
Let's pretend we wake up late on Wednesday mornings
and drink our coffee in bed.
Let's pretend, just for a moment,
that we stopped listening to other people,
but went ahead and followed our dreams anyway.
We stopped following their rules
and it turned out alright for us, in the end.
Let's pretend we're happy with the risk we took
because we were courageous
enough to follow our hearts
instead of
chasing
worried
voices.
Let's just pretend.

Face Your Fears

Confronting our enemies is an old tale,
written over and over again.
Our greatest challenges are not the battles against
those who defy us, but against those
who claim to love us,
yet steer us in the wrong direction,
time and time again.
Blood is thicker than friendships,
except for those who watch us bleed.

Change

I crave a change, wanting to feel excited again,
needing to feel like I somehow belong.

Wanting the world but too afraid to chase it.
All the doors are open but the hallways are dark.

How can I follow my path when I'm
choosing it blindly?
Wishing there was a hand to hold and follow me on this
journey, but everyone hides behind safe walls.

If we never make a change, we'll never know what
could be found behind the leaps and bounds of faith,
and courage.

Bare Branches

Stars shine and everything romantic is in between.
I've sung songs and played them on repeat,
while writing down your name in a notebook like a
teenage schoolgirl.

Hearts break but minds grow stronger.
Stars shine and everything is in between.
I loved you and never stopped to think if you loved me.

I bought the clock to count the seconds.
Leaves fell and I stopped thinking of you.

Bare branches bring comfort to my calmed soul.
They will bloom again.
I will, too.

Stay

Carry me home and stay a while.
Your other life can wait while you lay down next to me
and pretend we're a family.
I'll cook you dinner with your t-shirt on while you read
the newspaper and smile.
Stay a little while longer, just for tonight.
Tell your other life you won't make it home this time.
We can watch the moon
and stare into each other's eyes.
Let's pretend this is real and that I'll see you
lying next to me in the morning.
Just stay a little while.

Little One

Little one,
I can feel your unease as you make your way
into this big world.
You hesitate as you take each step,
with widened eyes
that cower from the journey ahead.

Little one,
although there may be plenty to fear,
most of the monsters that you hear about aren't real.
Have a little faith that I would never steer you wrong.
You'll soon wonder why you hadn't
explored the world in the first place.

Caves

I searched the deep, cavernous trenches in the coldest
parts of your soul,
looking for a homely fire, and a sign of love.
You have dug yourself so far down into the darkness
that it has swallowed you whole.
Drowning, sinking on a sturdy ship with holes.
You lost your magic somewhere along the way,
trying to redeem yourself of your past regrets.
Forgiving yourself is the beginning of healing
a broken mind,
when you're on the brink of madness.

Muse

My muse is not always a loving memory
or a longing stare.
Sometimes,
most times,
I am inspired by strong women who stand for their
beliefs against a world who told them they would never
rise from the ashes they were burned to.

Judgment Day

The real tragedy is how you spend your days
destroying yourself,
convinced you would never be good enough for them.
Judgmental minds shouldn't decide whether your
happiness lives or dies.

Butterfly

Wild wings
Flutter freely
As all
Untamed, unique
Creatures should

Unreturned

I sat at my empty table,
always saving your place,
hoping that you had finally learned how to love me.

The nights grew longer and your dinner got cold.
I smashed a plate at the thought of patiently waiting on
a love unreturned.
The only heart I need to mend is my own.

Old Ways

Old me, old ways.
I've been taking the old road home for years.
And I find myself feeling frustrated that I never felt a need to fit in.
I want to need the life you have,
but I've shielded myself with comfort
instead of popular styles.

I crossed your bridge.
New me, new ways.
I'm finally one of you,
but inside I've died.
Death will come early when you live to be
like everyone else.

Home

If you were to deep dive inside my mind,
you'd find that you have taken up a large portion
of my home.
I've hung up photographs of us and I've got your
favourite food in the fridge.
I have books on your accomplishments and fears, and
about all the things you love the most.
Being who you are, you have most definitely made it
into the hall of fame in the homes of others, and have
memories kept on their mantles.
No matter what house you've seen or been to,
I hope you'll move into mine for a little while longer.

Icy Waters

Haunted by the remnants of memories,
who I was seems so far away.
Photographs become a painful reminder that I am no longer the woman I worked so hard to be.
She was floating in the water, letting the sun's rays warm her face, as I continued to drown deeper into the depths of the oceans.
My surroundings grew colder and it felt like I was grasping at the air.
I mourned the loss of my old self,
but perhaps I was truly at fault for letting her slip away.

Queen of Hearts

Off with her head!
She's better off dead.
Her insides are filled with anger and dread.
Take her away and lock her right up.
Pour her some poison, in a dainty teacup.
That unpleasant girl, always wants more than is given.
Impatient and petulant, though she is driven
by unwavering thoughts of needing to be better.
Time is almost up, off to the cellar to chain her.
Off with her head!
She's better off dead.
The world cannot handle more powerful voices.
They would rather tread on their eggshells
and make easy choices.

Free

Abandoned on your doorstep,
wanting to fight for intertwined hands.
But he doesn't see you through rose coloured glasses
anymore.
You are internally bruised with harsh words
and a hungry stomach.
He wanted a perfect princess with pastel coloured shoes.
Tiptoeing around broken glass and bloodied floors.
You are wounded from battles and scarred from
fighting your way to the top.
You have been beaten down, mocked
and yelled at for nothing being
Woman enough.
Compliant enough.
Small enough.
You were not abandoned on your doorstep while
fighting for intertwined hands.
You were finally set free.

Answer the Door

Our desires are not handed to us on
gleaming silver platters,
or neatly laid out as we pick and choose
our pieces carefully.
They show up unexpectedly on our doorsteps.
no invitation required,
because life is as messy as dripping ice cream
on tiny hands,
leaving fingerprints on walls and carpets.
If we do not take advantage of strange opportunities,
we may never discover the butterfly
cocooned within them.

Silent Prayers

Sinking for months with no shore in sight,
drowning beneath layers of regret and sorrow.
I could see the sun but I never felt it.
Warm days are still cold when your heart is broken.
Eventually, the storm begins to subside,
and I eventually break the surface.
It had seemed like a lifetime that I hadn't felt
the tiny spark in my stomach
that ignites when I smile.
The Universe will answer the prayers you whisper
to yourself late at night,
wondering when you'll ever get the chance
to be happy again.

Ocean

Waking up in the middle of a sea storm,
waves crashing into me each time I gasp for air.
I am unable to reach the shore.
It seems so far away.
I let go in every dream,
surrendering to the murky waters letting myself sink.
Every night, I am back in the storm,
fighting for my life and some clarity;
why is my subconscious so damaged?
Night after night, it was always the same,
until finally one fateful day,
I was back in the ocean, but the water was clear.
The waves came crashing,
but hugged me,
letting me breathe beneath the tide.
The shore was closer, but I didn't need to reach it,
for I had become one with the waters,
knowing they would now take care of me.

Wishing Well

The old must be released so the new can enter.
Holding on to deadly thoughts because they bring
nostalgic comfort,
will keep you running on the same wheel,
caged up with the lock fastened tight.
Closing the door while staring out the window
will only bring sadness as you watch
everyone living their lives, unable
to walk your own path because
you're too afraid of falling down.
Scraped knees and cut elbows are part of the process.
Stop throwing coins and making passive wishes.
If you hit the bottom of the well,
there is only one way up.

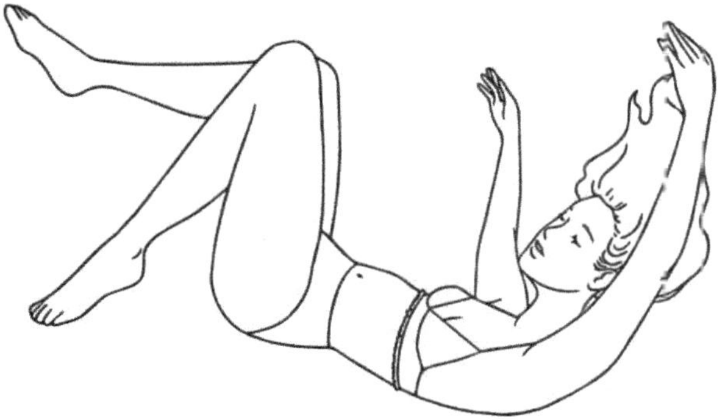

Firmly into the Ground

When something is right, it will hit you in the stomach,
full force.
It will flash its high beams and alert the press that you
are ready for this big step.
The naysayers may sway you in the direction less
wanted.
Plant your feet firmly into the ground beneath you,
covering your ears so they do not convince you that
your choices are wrong.
You know, deep down, that you are meant to take this
path, and the Universe
will knock anyone down
who tells you otherwise.

Simple Life

While you are wondering what it is, in this life,
you are meant for,
the answer is only a thought away.
What drives you to madness while you are
striving to achieve greatness?
What makes you wake up in the middle of the night,
questioning your every move?
What causes you to feel so deeply, that for a moment,
you wished you were just like everyone else -
that,
that is what you are meant for.
Stop spending your days staring at mundane people,
working simple jobs,
and then coming home to normal lives.
They have dinner and then watch television, because
their drive stops at the end of the street.
You are meant to turn this world upside down with
your visions and grace.
You were not destined to live a plain life.
So, start from within,
and conquer.

Voices

Surrounding you, are thousands of voices,
praising you for your dreams.
They scream that they wish they could
have your passion,
and believe in you.
You smile at them, staring into their hopeful eyes.
You crave their belief in you, because
you don't believe in yourself.
The thousands of voices surrounding you
become muffled as you walk away.
The only voice you hear in your head,
is the one who told you,
you wouldn't make it.

Teenage Universe

I swear the Universe is listening.
But sometimes,
it is as though she has on headphones,
with her music blaring,
while I am shouting at her for help.
Lucky moments aren't quite that
when they show up months later,
after the struggle has won.

Hotel Key

Frowns don't suit your face, especially
when I am the cause of them.
Being at the root of your unhappiness
destroys me internally.
You are not meant for mundane lifestyles
and pretty clothes.
I often wonder,
during my frequent sleepless nights,
if I am too modest in your grand hotel.
Every morning,
I try to be better for you,
but it seems I have lost
the hotel key.

Oak Tree

It is okay to change your mind
one too many times,
trying to determine how you will spend
the rest of your life.
You are allowed to jump around in all different places
until you find a cozy nook,
beneath a great oak tree,
that you can finally call home.

Matilda

Young Matilda was so vivacious.
She had stars in her eyes and diamonds in her hair.
She wore her extra pounds like a prized possession
as she stared at herself in the mirror
lovingly,
thinking and believing how pretty she looked tonight.

She walked around with her head held high,
with a confidence most envied.
She wore bright coloured shirts and tight blue jeans,
letting her hair flow to her waist,
thinking and believing how pretty she looked today.

Then one day, our poor Matilda's life took
a most unfortunate turn.
A small-minded little boy looked at her and said,
"Why Matilda, you could stand to be thinner."
Our confident Matilda never saw herself this way,
but today, she looked into the mirror and found a fault.

Years went by and the men were all the same.
Weighing her on the scale, her feet felt as though
they were lead.
They calculated her every move,
decided what she wore.
Matilda looked in the mirror, and this time,
she couldn't believe what she saw.

How could she have been so naive?
To think she was pretty all these years?

Her waist was too big and her legs were too wide.
Her nose was too long and her lips were too small.
Watching the tears roll down her face,
she wondered how she ever believed she was pretty.

Never fret, dear friends, for Matilda would soon find,
a knight in shining armor to save her from herself.
When you are sinking beneath the earth,
forgetting who you were before all of this began,
it can be hard to pull yourself out.

Our knight was not radiant, nor was he full of riches.
Instead, he was kind and patient.
He helped Matilda see who she was,
years before she believed small-minded lies,
and on one eventful day, Matilda looked in the mirror.
She was not fully content, and her smile wasn't as wide,
but she found that her waist was quite alright.
Her legs would do, and her nose wasn't so bad,
she actually liked the diamonds in her hair.
Matilda finally began to believe she was beautiful again.

Matilda forced herself to believe she was enough,
and lucky for her, our knight never gave up.
She is grown now, our young, brave Matilda,
and never, not for one second,
did she ever think of believing she was not pretty.

Fées

Faeries are never bothered by the world's disbelief,
which has no bearing on their true existence.
They flutter about, chuckling at monotonous adults,
while they sing songs with the witches in the forest.

Mondes merveilleux

Do not lose yourself in meaningless places,
only created to stunt your radiant growth.
Whatever your eyes rest upon
can create worlds of wonder.
The grass is greener because you are standing on it.

Old Jeans

Old jeans are not meant to fit years later.
You have outgrown negative mindsets and
toxic surroundings.
Old jeans serve as a reminder.
Toss them out and dance in flowing dresses
that allow you to breathe.

Fin

Thank you, once again, for joining me on this new
journey of ups and downs in love and in life.
We have travelled through the journal of my soul and
all of its emotional turmoil.
I hope you have found that we are not so different,
and that we can accomplish anything together.
I am right there with you.
There are seven billion people on this planet,
and we found a way to connect through emotion,
through heartbreak,
through love,
and most importantly,
through words.

Thank you.